Henry Westcott

Lexington centennial sermons

Delivered in the First Congregational Church

Henry Westcott

Lexington centennial sermons
Delivered in the First Congregational Church

ISBN/EAN: 9783337225032

Printed in Europe, USA, Canada, Australia, Japan

Cover: Foto ©Lupo / pixelio.de

More available books at **www.hansebooks.com**

LEXINGTON

CENTENNIAL SERMONS,

DELIVERED IN THE

FIRST CONGREGATIONAL CHURCH,

LEXINGTON, MASS.,

APRIL 11TH, 18TH, AND 25TH, 1875,

BY THE PASTOR,

Rev. HENRY WESTCOTT.

⸻ ⸻

›

BOSTON:
PRINTED BY FRANK WOOD, 352 WASHINGTON ST.
1875.

A SERMON

DELIVERED APRIL 11, 1875.

As the day which marks the close of a century since the beginning of the American Revolution approaches, no small amount of interest centres in the village of Lexington, which witnessed the opening scene of that war. Years ago, when, as school children, in some other town or State, many of us read the account of the "Battle of Lexington," it was with the resolution that, at some future day, our feet should stand upon the ground made sacred by the first blood shed in defence of American liberty. And now, when the day that many will choose on which to keep such resolutions is so near, let us glance hastily at the Old Lexington of pre-revolutionary times, and consider some of the causes which have made the name of our village familiar to every citizen of this country.

The feeling of interest which turns the thoughts of so many persons hither at the present time is not on account of any great battle, or of any superiority of the men who stood upon Lexington Green, waiting the approach of British soldiers. The "battle" was only a skirmish; and, had Gen. Gage sent his troops in any other direction, they would have found as brave men in every town as they found here. But Lexington Green happened to be the place where the British troops first met Americans in arms, drawn up for the express purpose of forcibly resisting, if possible, their movement of hostility. American blood had been shed as early as 1770, in Boston; and British blood had been shed in 1772, at the burning of the schooner Gaspee, in Narragansett Bay; and in other places blood had been shed previous to April 19, 1775. But in all these cases, the shedding of blood was occasioned by acts of annoyance on the part of the British, rather than by any act ·of direct hostility. Here, however, the British troops were on their way to strike a blow at the preparation which this colony was making for the conflict that was thought to be unavoidable. And the company on Lexington Green was, as Frothingham, in his " Siege of Boston," says, " a part of ' the constitutional army,' which was authorized to make a regular and forcible resistance to any open hostility by the British troops; and it was for this purpose that this gallant and devoted band on this memorable morning appeared on the field. Whether it ought to maintain its ground, or whether it ought to retreat, would depend upon the bearing and numbers of the regulars." Here the troops sent over to deprive these colonies of their liberties first came in conflict with a part of that army which had been raised to sustain those liberties. On account of the disproportion in numbers, the further march of the British was not prevented; but enough was done to awaken the spirit of resistance in the neighboring towns, and, indeed, in all the colonies. This is what gives, to-day, an interest in the name of Lexington.

The territory now included in the town of Lexington,

previous to the year 1713, formed a part of Cambridge, and was generally known as " Cambridge Farms." As it lay at some distance from the settlement of Cambridge, the land was taken up and built upon very slowly. For a long time, there was no central place of settlement. Here and there, as some adventurer found a tract of land to his liking, a house was built, and a home begun. In 1682, when the number of families had reached about thirty, the inconvenience of going from five to ten miles to the place of worship was felt to be so great that the people of this district petitioned the General Court to be set off as a distinct parish. On account of the opposition of the people of Cambridge, this was not effected until the year 1691, when the place was called North Cambridge. Immediately, the inhabitants made arrangements for building a meeting-house and securing a preacher. The meeting-house was built in 1692, and, for a time, Rev. Benjamin Estabrook was engaged from year to year to preach. In 1696, after providing him with a house, and arranging for a salary of forty-five pounds, they ventured to give him a call, which he accepted, being ordained in October of that year. Mr. Estabrook graduated at Harvard College in the year 1690, and was a young man of much promise, but he lived less than a year after his ordination.

The next minister was Rev. John Hancock, a graduate of Harvard College, who was settled in 1698. He was the grandfather of John Hancock, of Revolutionary fame; and he remained pastor of the church for fifty-five years.

Rev. Ebenezer Hancock, son of Rev. John Hancock,

was settled as colleague with his father in 1734, and died in 1740.

The inhabitants of this part of Cambridge in the early part of the eighteenth century had increased to such an extent, that they petitioned the General Court to be incorporated as a town, which petition was granted in the year 1713, the town taking the name of Lexington. As more than a score of cities, counties and towns in the United States have since received this name, it is a matter of interest to know where the name came from. The name, undoubtedly, came from Lord Lexington, of England, who was a noted man at the time of the incorporation of the town ; and was also a relation of Joseph Dudley, who was then Governor of the Province.

During the first half century which succeeded the incorporation of Lexington, the energies of the people were mainly devoted to the improvement of the town. Schoolhouses were built, schools were established, the support of the ministry was provided for, roads were opened, and many other things were attended to, which were required by a well-regulated and prosperous community. Some of the duties to which they attended seem strange to us, although they were regarded as important at that time. They appointed a committee to seat the families in the meeting-house according to age, dignity and wealth,—a duty which must have been very difficult to perform satisfactorily to all concerned. They appointed tythingmen to look after the children during and between the religious services on Sunday,— a task which could not have been a very easy one. Persons liable to become a public charge they warned out of town. In 1739, the town voted that representatives to the Great and General Court should serve for six shillings a day ; and in 1757, it was voted that all money received by the representatives over three shillings a day, should be paid into the town treasury.

Rev. Mr. Hancock died in the year 1752, and his funeral was something of public interest, so that the town made an appropriation to meet the expenses, and appointed a committee to take charge of the services. In 1761, the bell which gave the alarm on the morning of April 19, 1775, was presented to the town by Isaac Stone.

Although the citizens were devoted to the interests of the town, they were not backward in the support of the wars with the French and Indians. Whether the war was in the West Indies, or before Quebec or Louisburg, there were found representatives from this town. It was in such service as this, that the men of Lexington, and those of many other towns, learned the art of war, which they practised at a later period. It was by fighting by the side of British troops that they gained the courage to fight when opposed to them.

In 1755, Rev. Jonas Clark was ordained as the minister of the Lexington Church. Mr. Clark was a graduate of Harvard College, and he married a granddaughter of his predecessor, Rev. John Hancock. In the controversy between Great Britain and the American Colonies, which soon came to be the most important subject of thought, Mr. Clark took the greatest interest. As the controversy increased, Mr. Clark took a very active part in the proceedings of the town relating to that question. Most of the resolutions adopted by the citizens of the town expressing their views on the sub-

ject of the controversy were prepared by him. Edward
Everett said of those documents, "They have few equals,
and no superiors, among the productions of that class."
Weiss, in his life of Theodore Parker, says of Mr.
Clark: "He was more dangerous than all the military stores
at Concord or in the Colony, and had so infected the
whole district with his calm and deep indignation. v'iat,
when the regulars came marching up the old turnpike
in the gray dawn of the 19th of April, after powder and
flour, they found all the farmers converted to a doctrine
of liberty which armed and provisioned a young nation
for seven years of war."

I do not propose to discuss the causes of the American Revolution, but only to state the more immediate
measures on the part of Great Britain and the Colonies
which led to the conflict. In 1774, the British Parliament enacted laws by which certain officers, hitherto
chosen by the people, or representatives of the people,
in Massachusetts, were to be chosen by the king and
by the governor; and also forbidding all town meetings, except the annual ones, and all other public meetings, to be held, unless with the consent of the governor. This was virtually reducing the inhabitants of
the Colony to the condition of slaves. And it was the
attempt to enforce such laws, that led, by a direct path,
to an open conflict between the troops of Great Britain
and the Colonists. A meeting of delegates from the
Committees of Correspondence was held in Boston,
August 26 and 27, 1774. These delegates declared
that the inhabitants of the Colony "were entitled to
life, liberty, and the means of sustenance, by the grace
of Heaven and without the king's leave;" and resolved

that the officers who had been chosen according to the late act of Parliament ought to be resisted, that the military art ought attentively to be practised by the people, and that a " Provincial Congress is necessary for concerting and executing an effectual plan for counteracting the systems of despotism, and that each county will act wisely by choosing members as soon as may be for said congress, and by resolutely executing its measures when recommended." This was the first suggestion of a Provincial Congress; and the counties immediately began to act upon it by holding conventions, which advised the towns to choose delegates to such a body, and also passed determined and spirited resolutions.

September 1st, 1774, Gen. Gage summoned the General Court to meet at Salem on October 5th. On the 28th of September, he issued a proclamation excusing and discharging all who had been chosen representatives, and declaring his intention not to meet them. The reasons for this act were, "the many tumults and disorders which had taken place, the extraordinary resolves which had been passed in many of the counties, the instructions given by the town of Boston, and some other towns, to their representatives, and the disordered and unhappy state of the province." As a specimen of the spirit of those resolves which had intimidated the Governor, the Middlesex County Convention said : " If, in support of our rights, we are called upon to encounter death, we are yet undaunted, sensible that he can never die too soon, who lays down his life in support of the laws and liberties of his country." As a specimen of the instructions given by the towns to their representatives, Lexington instructed her representative, Jonas Stone, to " use his utmost influence that nothing be transacted as a court under the new council, or in conformity to any of the late acts of Parliament."

Notwithstanding the proclamation of Gen. Gage, nearly a hundred of the representatives met at Salem, October 5, and waited two days for the appearance of the Governor, who did not come. They therefore resolved themselves into a Provincial Congress, to be joined by such others as had been or should be chosen. The object of that Congress, as stated at the time, was : to " take into consideration the dangerous and alarming situation of public affairs in this province, and to consult and determine on such measures as they shall judge will tend to promote the true interest of his majesty, and the peace, welfare, and prosperity of the province."

The organization of this Provincial Congress was certainly the boldest step which had yet been taken. By such an organization, the inhabitants of this colony were resisting British authority, and were falling back upon the natural rights of man, just as truly as they were when they took up arms to resist British troops. The men who dared to sit in that Congress showed themselves as true heroes as did the men who shouldered their muskets and hastened to Lexington and Concord on the morning of the nineteenth of the following April. It is not strange, therefore, that Joseph Warren wrote to a friend about the members of that body : " You would have thought yourself in an assembly of Spartans, or ancient Romans, had you been a witness to the ardor which inspired those who spoke upon the important business they were transacting."

The proceedings of this Congress are of the utmost importance to every one who would understand the cause of the open acts of hostility which took place in the following spring. It was the work of this Congress and of the Committee of Safety which it appointed, that provoked Gen. Gage to send his troops on the expedition to Lexington and Concord ; and it was the work of this Congress and Committee that the inhabitants of this part of the province were prepared to meet those troops.

The Provincial Congress, after organizing at Salem, Oct. 7, adjourned to meet at Concord, Oct. 11. The Congress met at Concord, according to adjournment, and held there a session of four days. It adjourned Friday, Oct. 14, to meet at Cambridge on the following Monday, at which place all the remaining sessions of this first Provincial Congress were held. The second Provincial Congress also held its first session in Cambridge ; but on March 22, 1775, it met at Concord, where it continued in session till April 15. At the four days' session of the first Provincial Congress held at Concord, two important measures were adopted : an address to Governor Gage, which contained an account of the distresses, oppressions, and grievances to which the people were subjected, and a request that the Governor would desist from any further warlike preparations. The other important measure was the advising of the constables, collectors, and sheriffs not to pay any moneys in their hands to the treasurer of the province, but to retain the same until further advice from the Provincial Congress.

Among the important measures adopted by the first and second Congress while in session at Cambridge were the following : to purchase 20 field pieces, 4 mortars, 20 tons grape and round shot, 10 tons bomb shells, 5 tons lead balls, 1000 barrels of powder, 5000 arms and bayonets, and 75,000 flints; the appointment of a Committee of Safety, whose duties were to observe every attempt to invade or annoy the province, and, if necessary, to call out the militia; the people were urged to complete the organization of the military companies, to have them perfected in military discipline, and a part of them ready to march at the shortest notice.

"We think," said the Provincial Congress, "that particular care should be taken by the towns and districts in this colony, that each of the minute-men, not already provided therewith, should be immediately equipped with an effective fire-arm, bayonet, pouch, knapsack, thirty rounds of cartridges and balls, and that they be disciplined three times a week, and oftener as opportunity may offer." Besides this, the ministers of the colony were asked by Congress to advise their congregations to adhere strictly to the resolutions of the Continental Congress. The church at Cambridge in which the Provincial Congress held its sessions when these and many other important measures which led to the beginning of open hostilities were adopted, no longer stands. Were it standing, there would be no other building in this country to which pilgrimages would more readily be made by citizens of the United States.

When we remember that the measures and resolutions which were adopted by the Provincial Congress, were sup. plemented by the earnest action of the Committees of Safety and Supplies in procuring field-pieces, muskets, balls, cartridges, powder, bayonets, tents, provisions, and medicines — every thing that an army in actual service could possibly require — and concealing them at Concord and Worcester, we can understand something of the feelings with which our forefathers passed through those months during which the Provincial Congress was in session. Everywhere in the province was seen a preparation for war. But probably nowhere was there more interest taken in that preparation than in the towns which were in the neighborhood of Cambridge, where the Provincial Congress was in session, and Boston, where the British troops were quartered. In the records of every town are found the evidences of this interest. If we look in the records of this town, we find the citizens during those months holding frequent town meetings, and voting to provide flints, and bayonets, and drums, and all other things necessary for a forcible resistance of British troops. As a year previous to this time, they had resolved that " we trust in God, that should the state of our affairs require it, we shall be ready to sacrifice our estates and everything dear in life, yea, and life itself, in support of the common cause," so at the time we are considering, they were making active preparations to fulfil their promise to sustain the common cause, which they then saw clearly must be done, with the sacrifice of their lives. We are so accustomed to dwell upon the events of the nineteenth of April, 1775, that we fail to realize the anxiety in which the few months previous to that time were passed by the inhabitants of this town. With what eagerness must they have looked for each measure adopted by the Provincial Congress, and with what anxiety must they have heard of every movement of the troops at Boston. As the winter wore away with the increasing certainty of the approaching conflict, and as the spring opened with the Provincial Congress meeting in March, at Concord, to perfect the work of preparation which it had previously laid out; as the days passed by, with the conflict apparently so near that men were appointed to watch closely every movement of the British, there must have been many anxious hearts within this town. Nearly every family had one or more of its members enrolled in the military company of the town; and for many nights husbands, and wives, and children, and fathers, and mothers, must have fallen asleep, expecting, before morning, to hear the alarm rung out from the belfry on the Green. At last, the alarm was heard. About one o'clock, on the morning of the 19th of April, 1775, the inhabitants of Lexington who dwelt along the road leading to Boston heard the clattering of a horse's hoofs. It was the horse of Paul Revere, who was hastening with a message from Joseph Warren, to Samuel Adams and John Hancock, who were passing the night with Rev. Jonas Clark, that a large body of the King's troops were embarked in boats from Boston, and that it was suspected they were ordered to destroy the stores at Concord. Soon the bell sounded the alarm, and by two o'clock, nearly all the members of Capt. Parker's company answered to their names, as the roll was called upon the Green

If it be asked, For what did these men meet upon the Green? the answer is given by Rev. Mr. Clark, in his narrative of the events of that day. It was " not with any design of *commencing hostilities* upon the *King's troops*, but to consult what might be done for our own and the people's safety : And also to be ready for whatever service Providence might call us out to upon this alarming occasion, in case *overt acts* of *violence* or *open* hostilities should be committed." And he further says : " From a most intimate acquaint ance with the sentiments of the inhabitants of this town then collected in arms, I think I may boldly assert that it was their *known* determination not to com mence hostilities upon the king's troops ; though they were equally determined to stand by their rights to the last." Capt. Parker's company remained upon the Green about an hour, when, hearing nothing of the regulars, the company was dismissed, with orders to appear immediately at the beat of the drum. Some of the members, whose homes were near, retired thither, while the greater part went into Buckman's tavern, which stood on the opposite side of the road.

I wish we had the tales of that wayside inn ; that we knew of what those men talked while they awaited the roll of the drum which should call them again into line. They were subjects of George III., yet they were sup plied with powder and balls, and had their muskets loaded, in expectation of the coming of the king's troops. Although all the inhabitants of the colony had been looking forward to this, their position—the king's subjects in arms against the king's troops—was a strange one, and it must have seemed so to them.

Doubtless they discussed the last measures of the Provincial Congress, of the Committee of Safety, of the Committee of Supplies, the latest news about the British in Boston, the prospect of a war and its probable results, and the object of the military expedition which they had been called out to watch, and, if possible, oppose. No doubt there were as patriotic sentiments uttered in that wayside inn on that night as had been heard in the churches at Cambridge and Concord from members of the Provincial Congress. Doubtless they strengthened each other's hearts with assertions of their readiness to meet the troops of the king, and with determined resolutions that George III., Lord North, and the Parliament should be taught a lesson long to be remembered. If the walls of that building could only speak and tell what occurred during that hour when those " village Hampdens " sat and talked in the light of the cheerful fire, the story would be one of the most interesting relics to be shown on the coming anniversary.

But their conversation and discussions were suddenly interrupted by the roll of the drum and the alarm gun. Grasping their muskets, and taking one look at them to see if they were ready for resistance, should it be necessary, they hastened from the house, and to the Green. There, while they were forming in line, — before the line was completely formed, — the British troops made their appearance between the meeting-house and the tavern. Captain Parker ordered every man to stand his ground, but not to fire unless fired upon. Pitcairn, the commanding officer of the British, shouted to the Minute-men, " Lay down your arms and

disperse, you rebels!'' and then immediately ordered
his troops to "Fire!" at the same time firing his own
pistol. The British fired, first over the heads of the
Minute-men ; but at the second command, they fired and
killed and wounded a number of the Americans. Seeing his men outnumbered, Parker ordered them to disperse. But before obeying that order, some of the
company returned the fire, and others, while dispers-
ing, did the same. The British continued pursuing
and firing, until all who were alive had escaped. Then
the troops gave three huzzas, and proceeded towards
Concord, leaving eight Americans killed, and nine
wounded, and having had two or three of their men
wounded. Such is an account of the fight or skirmish
at Lexington, on the morning of April 19, 1775, as accepted by all historians.

The news of what had been done reached Concord
before the British did. The neighboring towns also
had been alarmed, and men from Acton and Lin-
coln stood with those of Concord to offer further resistance. While a part of the British troops were engaged
in searching for and destroying stores, a detachment
left to guard the North bridge fired upon the Americans, who outnumbered the British, three to one. They
returned the fire, killing one and wounding a number
of the regulars. The British that were at North
bridge retreated towards the centre of the town, and
joined the main body of their troops ; and soon the
whole body began that retreat which proved so disas-
trous to them, all the way from Concord, through Lexington and Arlington, to Charlestown.

In regard to what took place on Lexington Green in

the morning, attempts have been made within the past fifty years to raise a question, whether or no the minute-men returned the fire of the British troops. But there never was any such question to be raised. There is no more doubt that the minute-men on Lexington Green returned the fire of the British, than there is that the minute-men were on the Green. The testimony which conflicts with this statement was not such, either in amount or character, as caused the shadow of a doubt in the minds of the members of the Provincial Congress that the fire of the British was returned. The narrative of the events of April 19, ordered by the Provincial Congress to be published in the following month, implies that the fire was returned by the Americans, in the statement, that the British "first began the hostile scene, by firing on this small party, by which they killed eight men on the spot, and wounded several others, before any guns were fired upon the troops by our men." In the proclamation of the Provincial Congress of June 16, 1775, it is expressly stated that the fire of the British was returned. "The fire was returned by some of the survivors," are the words employed. Gordon, who visited Lexington and Concord a few days after the battle, ascertained, both from the Americans and from British prisoners, that the minute-men did return the fire. Rev. Jonas Clark, of Lexington, in his narrative of the events of the day, says: "Very few of our people fired at all; and even they did not fire till, after being fired upon by the troops, they were wounded themselves, or saw others killed or wounded by them, and looked upon it next to impossible for them to escape." This is what the

earliest authorities say ; and it has been accepted by all
historians from that time to this ; the last historian,
Higginson, whose book was published only a few weeks
ago, saying distinctly: "The Americans fired in return."
And I am not aware that there was ever any pretence
of a doubt about this, till half a century had passed
away. There is no fact concerning the whole American
Revolution which has much better authentication than
the fact that on Lexington Green *began* that resistance
to British troops which was continued at Concord,
which was continued all the way from Concord to
Charlestown, which was continued at Bunker Hill,
which was continued till 1783, when the British troops
were driven from American soil, and the liberties of
the American colonies were secured.

It is true that the firing by the minute-men on Lexington Green was not done in obedience to any command
of Capt. Parker. Individual soldiers fired upon their
own responsibility. But I am not aware that that circum-
stance detracts from the significance or importance of
the firing. There was very little firing by the Americans
on that day that was done in obedience to the commands of officers. It was done by individuals behind trees,
fences and walls. If the firing of the Americans on
Lexington Green was not of much importance, then
there was very little firing of importance done on that
day, and the approaching celebration of the centennial
anniversary of that day can be scarcely anything more
than a farce.

It may be asked, What was gained by the resistance
made on Lexington Green ? A few men died a glorious
death, but the expedition of the British was detained

only about half an hour. What advantage was gained
by the Colonies from the death of the men whose dust
reposes under yonder monument? Some defeats effect
more than some victories. The battle of Bunker Hill was
not a victory for the Americans; yet no one will deny
that it exerted a great influence in favor of the Americans. It must be remembered that the organization of
the Minute-men throughout this Colony was for the purpose of resisting any open acts of hostility on the part of
the British. While the Colonists were determined not to
be the aggressors, they were equally determined to oppose every open act of British hostility. Word came
to Lexington that the British troops had left Boston
that evening, evidently with hostile intentions. Samuel
Adams, John Hancock, Paul Revere, and Jonas Clark·
were right when they decided that it was the duty of
the Minute-men of Lexington to be prepared for any
service that might be required. It was no uncertain
sound that came from that belfry on the Green. It said
plainly that, if the British meant war, it might begin
here.

On the monument at Thermopylæ, which marked
the spot where a few Greeks allowed themselves to be
sacrificed by the overwhelming hosts of the Persian in-
vader, the poet wrote the words: —

> "Stranger, the tidings to the Spartan tell,
> That here, obeying their commands, we fell."

It was the same message that went forth on that
morning of April 19, 1775, from this field of blood, to
the inhabitants of this Colony. Obeying the commands
of the people of this Colony, as expressed by their Con-

gress, those men fell on Lexington Green. And had there been no further resistance on that day, their blood would have been enough to summon the people of this and all the other Colonies to arms, and to drive those who were worse than invaders from the land Truly said Jonas Clark, "The innocent blood of our brethren was the cement of the Union, and seal of the freedom of these American States! All America heard the alarm, deeply felt the wound, and bravely rose to revenge their brethren's blood, and join the common cause."

-It should not be our endeavor, at this time, to exalt our town on account of what was done here a century ago. They of that time said, "Not unto us, O Lord, but unto thee be the glory ; " and in this let us follow their example. Let us be content with the position which history accords to the heroes of that morning, and to the soil on which they fell. Bancroft says of the men who fell at that time, "These are the village heroes, who were more than of noble blood, proving by their spirit that they were of a race divine. They gave their lives in testimony to the rights of mankind, bequeathing to their country an assurance of success in the mighty struggle which they began. Their names are held in grateful remembrance, and the expanding millions of their countrymen renew and multiply their praise from generation to generation." Of these men Everett said : "To the end of time, the soil whereon ye fell is holy ; and shall be trod with reverence, while America has a name among the nations." And of the citizens of Lexington he said, "On their soil, and on that day, commenced the dread appeal to arms, long

anticipated, though loyally deprecated by the friends
of American liberty. On that day, and on their soil,
commenced the struggle in which so much hardship
was endured, and so much precious blood was shed,
and which, by the blessing of Providence, was con-
ducted by the Heaven-appointed chieftain to its auspi-
cious result." But whatever may be said of those men,
or of the ground on which they fell, let us remember
that it was not for the glory of this town that they
died. As we consider the spirit by which they were
inspired, the names of men and towns sink out of sight
in the noble cause in which they were engaged. Let
us not look back to that day saying, " What a day for
the glory of Lexington!" but " What a glorious day
for *America!*"

A SERMON DELIVERED APRIL 18th, 1875.

Psalm XXXIII. 12.

"BLESSED IS THE NATION WHOSE GOD IS THE LORD."

Before the Pilgrims and the Puritans set their feet upon the shores of New England, they expressed their purpose in coming hither, in a way which assures us that they intended to found a nation whose God should be the Lord. In the cabin of the "Mayflower," the Pilgrims signed a compact, a part of which is: "We, whose names are underwritten, having undertaken, for the glory of God, and advancement of the Christian faith, and honor of our king and country, a voyage to plant the first colony in the northern parts of Virginia, do, by these presents, solemnly and mutually, in the presence of God and one of another, covenant and combine ourselves together into a civil body politic, for our better ordering and preservation, and furtherance of the ends aforesaid." During the voyage of the ship "Arbella," which brought over the Puritans, Gov. Winthrop wrote a treatise, in which he stated that the work they had in hand was, "by a mutual consent, through a special, over-ruling Providence, and a more than an ordinary approbation of the churches of Christ, to seek out a place of cohabitation and consortship under a due form of government, both civil and ecclesiastical." Both colonies attempted to carry this theory of government into practice, the Puritans making the right of franchise dependent upon church-membership. It was by them "ordered and agreed, that, for the time to come, no man shall be admitted to the freedom of this body politic but such as are members of some of the churches within the limits of the same." And in order that this should not be evaded by the organization of churches which were churches only in name, it was ordered by the General Court that it " doth not, nor will hereafter, approve of any such companies of men as shall henceforth join in any pretended way of church-fellowship, without they shall first acquaint the magistrates and the elders of the greater part of the churches in this jurisdiction with their intentions, and have their approbation therein. And further, it is ordered, that no person being a member of any church which shall hereafter be gathered without the approbation of the magistrates and the greater part of the said churches, shall be admitted to the freedom of this Common-wealth." As Palfrey says : " They established a kind of aristocracy hitherto unknown. Not birth, nor wealth, nor learning, nor skill in war, was to confer political power ; but personal character, — goodness of the highest type, — goodness of that purity and force which only the faith of Jesus Christ is competent to create." I do not propose to discuss the question whether such theories of government as these, or such legislation, were or were not wise. But I bring these facts forward to show the spirit with which our fore-fathers came to this country, and also the spirit with which they worked in building up a nation. They believed that they were as truly called to go out from England to a land that God would show them, as did Abraham that he was called to go out from his country. They as firmly believed that they were building up a nation in this country, whose God was the Lord, as did the descendants of Abraham in the land of Palestine. If we sometimes think that this feeling was too strong for the good of the aborigines, we must remember also, that without some such feeling as this they would not have braved all the danger and sufferings that they did in order to build up a nation. And the same belief, that in some way God was the Lord and the Protector of this people, was not extinguished with the generation which came to these shores. Their children and their children's children received such a belief for their inheritance. Religion was the spirit and the life of these colonies, flowing into the trunk and branches. Not only did the nation have its root in religion, and its trunk supported by it, but every branch which pushed out into the wilderness bore on it the bud which was to unfold into a church. Thus it was in the settlement of Lexington, then called Cambridge Farms. Houses were built, scattered here and there, the inhabitants going to the settlement at Cambridge to worship. But as soon as the number of families was large enough to make a church of themselves, there was a petition to be considered as a distinct parish. It was the church idea, the need of worship, which first suggested the thought of separation from the parent town of Cambridge. And when, in the middle of the eighteenth century, the controversy with Great Britain arose, and the dark war-cloud loomed up above the eastern horizon, the people of these colonies,—of the New England colonies especially,—believed that the controversy was one in which the Supreme Ruler had an interest ; and if it were to be decided by an appeal to arms, they might place their reliance upon that God who was the Lord of the nation. For this reason, the questions at issue were discussed over and over again in the pulpits of the land. If there was to be a war, it would be a religious war, as truly as were the wars of Joshua. And thus church and state were united. Election sermons were printed, and circulated as political tracts. The fire of patriotism which burned so brightly in the hearts of the people was kindled by a coal from the altar of God. Headley says : " The teachings of the pulpit of Lexington caused the first blow to be struck for American Independence." But the blows which were struck for American Independence would have been far fewer and far feebler, had it not been for patriotic teachers in *most* of the pulpits of these colonies.

In December, 1774, when the Boston Port Bill was in operation, and when the prospect for the approaching winter was very dark, the Provincial Congress appealed to the ministers to aid in the common cause. " In a day like this," they said, " when all the friends of civil and religious liberty are exerting themselves to deliver this country from its present calamities, we cannot but place great hope in an order of men who have ever distinguished themselves in their country's cause ; and do thereby recommend to the ministers of the gospel in the several towns and other places in this colony, that they assist us in avoiding that dreadful slavery with which we are now threatened, by advising the people of their several congregations, as they wish their prosperity, to abide by, and strictly adhere to, the resolutions of the Continental Congress." And to the inhabitants of this colony, the Provincial Congress could say : " Let nothing unbecoming our character as Americans, as citizens and Christians, be justly chargeable to us. Whoever considers the number of brave men inhabiting North America, will know that a general attention to military discipline must so establish their rights and liberties, as under God to render it impossible to destroy them." Thus did the Provincial Congress, the very first political body created solely by the inhabitants of this colony, acknowledge their obligations as Christians, and their dependence upon God.

If we look at the election sermons delivered a few years before the commencement of hostilities, we shall find the doctrine of resistance to tyranny very plainly stated. In 1771, Rev. John Tucker, of Newbury, preached the election sermon before Gov. Hutchinson, the Council and House of Representatives, in which he said : " Proper submission in a free state is a medium between slavish subjection to arbitrary claims of Rulers, on one hand, and a lawless license on the other. It is obedience in subjects to all orders of government which are consistent with their constitutional rights and privileges. So much submission is due, and to be readily yielded by every subject ; and beyond this, it cannot be justly demanded, because Rulers and people are equally bound by the fundamental laws of the constitution." Here was the doctrine on which the colonists based their right of resistance, promulgated from the pulpit four

years before the Revolution. In 1773, Rev. Charles
Turner, in the Election Sermon, said : " When the civil
rights of a country receive a shock, it may justly render the ministers of God deeply thoughtful for the safety
of sacred privileges—for religious liberty is so blended
with civil, that if one falls it is not to be expected that
the other will continue." In 1774, when matters
seemed to be drawing to a crisis, the preacher of the
Election sermon, Rev. Gad Hitchcock, of Pembroke,
spoke in still bolder words from the text, " When the
righteous are in authority the people rejoice, but when
the wicked bear rule the people mourn." " Our danger
is not visionary, but real ; our contention is not about
trifles, but about liberty and property, and not ours
only, but those of posterity to the latest generation. If
I am mistaken in supposing plans are formed and executing, subversive of our natural and chartered rights
and privileges, and incompatible with every idea of
liberty, *all America is mistaken with me.* Our continued complaints, our repeated humble, but fruitless,
unregarded petitions and remonstrances, and if I may
be allowed the sacred allusion, our groanings that cannot be uttered, are at once indications of our sufferings,
and the feeling sense we have of them. Let the Governor in his chair of state hear it : we not only mourn,
but with groanings that cannot be uttered, and all
because *the wicked rule.* The castle cannot shelter him
from that scorching thunderbolt. Families are divided,
brother is arrayed against brother, friend against friend.
Society is cut from its moorings, and hate and conster-
nation reign on every side, and all because *the wicked
bear rule.* King George may say the evils that produce

this state of things are imaginary; but I tell you, and I tell the tyrant to his face, it is because *the wicked bear rule.*" When such sermons as these were preached, it is not surprising that the Governor, in 1774, refused to appoint a fast : " For the request," he said, " was only to give an opportunity for sedition to flow from the pulpit." On account of the sufferings of the Boston people in the year 1774, occasioned by the enforcement of the Port Bill, the ministers of Connecticut wrote to the ministers of Boston : " The taking away of civil liberty will involve the ruin of religious liberty also. Bear your heavy load with Christian fortitude and resolution." From the Boston ministers went back the answer : " While we complain to Heaven and earth of the cruel oppression we are under, we ascribe righteousness to God. The surprising union of the colonies affords encouragement. It is an inexhaustible source of comfort that the Lord omnipotent reigneth." Thus there was in the minds of the people, underneath the thought of independence, the thought that the spirit of the church and the state are one ; that religious liberty and civil liberty must stand or fall together. If the inhabitants of these colonies believed they had the right to stand up for their liberties, it was because they regarded those liberties as the gift of God, of which not even kings or any earthly authorities had the right to deprive them.

It is impossible for the inhabitants of this town to think of the union of religion and government, without having their thoughts turn to the man who, one hundred years ago, was pastor of this church and society, the Rev. Jonas Clark. There is no other name connected

with Lexington that better deserves honorable mention,
at this centennial anniversary, than his. And here
to-day, among the members of this religious society, of
which he was once the pastor, all our thoughts of him
must be tinged with a peculiar feeling of reverence.
There is only one thing that we can see which remains
to-day to recall his name and memory. The old
church in which he preached is gone. Of those who
formed his congregation, none remain. Only this Bible
remains. It was presented to this society by Gov.
John Hancock, in the year 1793, and during the last
twelve years of the life of Mr. Clark, it was used by
him in the religious services of the society. His hands
have turned over its leaves. His voice has been heard
speaking words of sacred wisdom as his eyes rested
upon its pages. It is a precious relic.

But, if there were nothing outward remaining to
remind us of him, still his name could not possibly be
forgotten on such an occasion as this, nor the spirit of
the man be remembered without the utmost reverence.
Mr. Clark was pastor of this society during a period of
fifty years and ten days, having been ordained November 5, 1755, and having died November 15, 1805.
Had nothing unusual occurred in this colony during
those fifty years, Mr. Clark would have been remembered as an earnest preacher, a devoted pastor, and a
man of "strong sense and sound judgment." "His
public discourses," it is said, " consisted not of learned
discussions on speculative or metaphysical subjects,
nor yet of dry lectures on heathen morality, but of the
most interesting truths of the gospel, well arranged for
the edification of his hearers. And they were delivered

not in a formal, heartless manner, but with uncommon
energy and zeal." But, living as he did during a peculiar period, requiring peculiar talents, he showed himself
equal to the emergency. Church and state were united
in him. He was not only a minister but a statesman.
Probably no one understood the questions at issue between the colonies and the mother country better than
he. And his people received the benefit of his states-
manship, not only in their town meetings, but from the
pulpit. "Enough of his discourses," says a descend-
ant of his, "have been preserved to make it plain
what, on a thousand occasions long before even the
passage of the Stamp Act, would have been the strain
of his thought and of his speech; so that, when the
struggle actually commenced, the people were ready
for it, thoroughly acquainted with the reasons on which
the duty of resistance was founded, and prepared to
discharge the duty at every hazard. No single individual probably did so much to educate the people up to
that point of intelligence, firmness and courage, as their
honored and beloved pastor." In one of his sermons,
Mr. Clark thus illustrated the necessity of religion to
government: "In civilized nations, and where civil
government hath been established, many cities and
places of importance may be found without walls, without guards, and even without weapons or any preparations for common defence. But it is not easy to find
any without a temple, an altar, a grove, or some other
place appointed and appropriated to the purpose of
religion, the acknowledgment of Heaven, and the worship of the Deity, in some shape or other." It is well
known that Mr. Clark drew up most of the important

political papers and resolutions, in regard to the great question at issue, which were adopted by the town of Lexington. There can be no doubt that the men who assembled on Lexington Green, on the morning of April 19th, 1775, were there to make a practical application of the doctrine which they had heard enforced in the church. Robert Munroe, Jonas Parker, Samuel Hadley, Jonathan Harrington, Isaac Muzzy, Caleb Harrington, and John Brown, who were slain on that morning, doubtless felt that, if their lives were sacrificed, they would be offered up, not only on the altar of their country, but on the altar of their God. Of their country and their God they could truly say, "To die for her is serving Thee." And this feeling was not confined to this town. Everywhere men looked upon the war as a holy war. They believed that when they took their muskets and hastened to the conflict, they were engaged in a religious act, just as truly as when they met to worship God. They went into the war, feeling, as David had said : "The Lord is on my side; I will not fear ; what can man do unto me?" "Call me an enthusiast," said Samuel Adams ; "this union among the colonies, and warmth of affection, can be attributed to nothing less than the agency of the Supreme Being. If we believe that he superintends and directs the affairs of empires, we have reason to expect the restoration and establishment of the public liberties."

Headley says: " In every quiet little valley and sequestered nook in New England, the pastor had taught the doctrines of freedom, and preached the duty of resistance to oppression. The farmers and mechanics listened with reverence and confidence to these teachings, and showed their faith by their works when the hour of trial came. At the battle-cry that rolled over the land from Lexington and Concord, they shouldered their muskets, and went forth with the blessing of their pastor on their heads, and his fervent prayers for their success following their footsteps. They had been taught from the pulpit that it was the cause of God, and they took it up in the full belief that they had his blessing and his promise. If the scenes that transpired in the countless villages and hamlets of New England, when the news of the first blood shed by British troops swept over the colonies, and the first uprising of the people took place, could be described just as they occurred, in all the beauty, pathos, patriotism and religion that characterized them, the Revolutionary struggle would possess an interest that all its thrilling battles and perilous marches, deeply as they enlist our sympathies, can never impart." The historian describes one such scene, in Stockbridge, at which place the news of the Lexington and Concord fight arrived on Sunday forenoon. Signal shots were immediately fired, and men who were preparing to go to the house of worship took down their firelocks, bid their families farewell, and hastened to the yard of the deacon, the appointed place of meeting. The old pastor came and stood among them, reading from his Bible, offering a prayer, imparting his blessing, and then "twenty men, with knapsacks on their backs, and muskets on their shoulders, started on foot for Boston, nearly two hundred miles distant."

So it was throughout a great part of the colonies. Whether men waited or not for religious services, they all went forth with the same spirit,—that their cause was just because it was the cause of God. Though in the midst of oppression and distress, they believed that a blessing was awaiting the nation because the God of the nation was the Lord.

A part of the text of the sermon preached in Lexington in 1779, on the anniversary of the battle, was " Hitherto hath the Lord helped us." At the centennial anniversary of the incorporation of the town, Rev. Mr. Williams, then pastor of this society, preached a discourse, with the same text : " Hitherto hath the Lord helped us." And now that we have come to the centennial anniversary of the battle of Lexington, can we say the same thing of our nation : "Hitherto hath the Lord helped us?" Looking around us now, and looking as far into the future as possible, can we say, Blessed is *this* nation, whose God is the Lord? Have we any of that old faith of our forefathers left? Have we any faith that God cares for this nation, in the least? Whether we have any of that faith or not, I believe we ought to have. It may be necessary to modify it somewhat; but there is a faith in national dependence upon God which no nation should be without. I am aware that men with little or no religious spirit may say that such a faith was an illusion with our forefathers ; and they may add that it was also an illusion with the Jews, who, although firmly believing that the God of their nation was the Lord, and that their nation was to be blessed on that account, yet saw their nation, as a nation, utterly destroyed. If those words are true, " Blessed is the nation whose God is the Lord," why was it, they will ask, that there was such a sad end to the Jewish nation, which, before all other nations, claimed to recognize the Lord as its God ? The answer to that question will lead us to the true faith of national dependence upon God.

The Jews were fond of calling themselves the chosen people of God; but they forgot in the later period of their history that there could be a nation chosen by God in any abitrary manner. They forgot that there could be any chosen people of God, except as they obeyed the commandments of God; they forgot the words which Moses had spoken to the nation : "The Lord thy God hath chosen thee to be a special people unto himself. Thou shalt, therefore, keep the commandments and the statutes, and the judgments which I command thee this day. Wherefore it shall come to pass if ye keep and do them, that the Lord thy god will love thee and bless thee, and thou shalt be blessed above all people. But it shall be, if thou do at all forget the Lord thy God and walk after other Gods, and serve them and worship them, I testify against you this day, that ye shall surely perish." That is the faith of national dependence upon God that Moses taught.

It was the same theory of national dependence upon God that the prophet Jeremiah taught the stubborn Jews in the parable of "The Potter." "I went down to the potter's house, and, behold, he wrought a work on the wheels. And the vessel that he made of clay was marred in the hands of the potter ; so he made it again another vessel, as it seemed good to the potter to make it. Then the word of the Lord came to me, saying, O house of Israel, cannot I do with you as this potter ? saith the Lord. Behold as the clay is in the potter's hand, so are ye in mine hands, O house of Israel." That does not mean that God governs the nations arbitrarily, but rather in accordance with certain laws. As F. W. Maurice said : " When Jeremiah was sent to study the potter's work, he was sent to ascertain, not what the potter might do if he liked, but *what* he liked. He desired to make a vessel of a certain form. That was the end for which he labored. If there is any force or worth in the analogy at all, it must mean that there is a form according to which God is seeking to mould men and nations. It must imply that he is not doing any single act arbitrarily, or without reference to a purpose ; it must imply that he is patiently, continually working for the accomplishment of this purpose ; and if they do not submit to this process, if they persist in not taking the mould which he would give them, then the clay is broken that it may be re-formed, that the original intent of the owner may still be carried out."

John the Baptist taught the same doctrine to the Pharisees and Sadducees : " Think not to say within yourselves, we have Abraham to our father ; for I say unto you that God is able of these stones to raise up children unto Abraham." And to the hardened Jews who resisted the truth, but said, "Abraham is our father," the Saviour taught the same doctrine : " If ye were Abraham's children ye would do the works of Abraham." But the teachings of patriarch, prophet, and of the Saviour could avail nothing. The recognition of the Lord as their God was only in name with the Jews. There was no reality in it.. And the sins of that people led, by direct laws, established by God, to destruction.

In the hands of God are all the nations of the earth. There may be a chosen nation now, just as truly as there ever was. But the chosen nation is the nation which keeps the divine laws, and obeys the divine commands. " Blessed is the nation whose God is the Lord ; " not in name, merely, but in truth. And God blesses nations for obedience, not arbitrarily, as you reward a boy for doing an errand. But the laws of God are such that national strength is the result of obedience, and national weakness is the result of disobedience. It is possible to trace the connection between the immorality, the disobedience of the commands of God of some of the ancient nations, and the weakness which resulted in their downfall. It is sometimes said of nations that they have their period of rising, and their period of degeneration and overthrow, as if it were an invariable rule. But if it seem so, it is because there never has been a nation capable of resisting the temptations of prosperity. "Righteousness," it is said, "exalteth a nation, but sin is a reproach to any people." So long as a nation keeps in the path of righteousness, so long it will be blessed by God, so long will it have strength to remain a nation. I do not mean that righteousness alone will maintain a place for any people among the nations of the earth. There are other requisites for national existence than righteousness, or obedience of divine laws. But when all these requisites exist in a nation, righteousness will tend to strengthen and perpetuate it, and unrighteousness will tend to weaken and overthrow it.

If we ask ourselves, what will be the future of our country, let us remember that we are not a chosen people

or a favored nation now, because we had the Pilgrims
and the Puritans for our fathers. We can see how
their virtues made them strong, and how the virtues
of the colonists, a century ago, also made them strong.
But unless we also have their virtues, we can not rely
upon our ancestors for our national strength to-day. If
there is anything which threatens the overthrow of this
nation to-day, if there is anything at which thoughtful
men may feel alarmed, it is the neglect of some of those
stern virtues of our fathers which we affect to despise.
I do not wish to see church and state united as it was
with the Puritans. Their religious test was a failure,
so far as keeping bad men out of office was concerned.
But never was there a time when we could see plainer
than now, that our continued prosperity depends on
placing men in office possessing the principles which
Christianity inculcates. When a foreigner can write
about us as Strauss, the German, has written, it is time
for us to try and see ourselves as others see us. "The
air of the United States," he says, "is infected by a
corruption of its leading classes, only to be paralleled in
the most abandoned parts of Europe. The practice in
their presidential elections, the inevitable corruption
following in their wake, the necessity of rewarding the
accomplices by giving them places, and then of winking
at the delinquencies of their administration, the venality
and corruption which are thus engendered in the ruling
circles,—all these deep-lying evils of the much-vaunted
republic have been brought into such glaring promi-
nence within the last few years, that the eagerness of
German orators, newspapers, writers, and poets, to go in
search of their political, and even moral ideals to the

other side of the Atlantic Ocean, has suffered consider-
able abatement." We may pretend to despise all such
foreign criticism as that, but we cannot deny that there
is a vein of truth in it. And we may be sure that when
we cease to be an ideal example for every individual in
all nations who is looking toward freedom, we have
not only ceased to perform one of our most important
missions, but we are losing that element of grandeur
and of strength which has hitherto given us an exalted
place among the nations of the earth.

But although there is evidently danger in this direction, I cannot despair of the final result. Although there
are thousands of politicians who think that trickery and
bribery, and corruption, so long as they aid their party,
are perfectly innocent, still there are others, who know
that these things are sapping the foundations of the
government. And there is no small amount of the spirit
of the Pilgrims and Puritans and colonists still remaining
among us, which holds that disobedience of the laws of
God will work injury to the nation. That spirit is patient
and long-suffering under distress and oppression ; but if
national evils continue to increase, that spirit will ere
long prompt men to join hands and drive corrupt politicians from the government, as it inspired men a century
ago to band together, and drive the British from
America. It looks now as if, before long, party plat-
forms will be planed down, till nothing remains but
questions of truth, honesty and purity ; and when it
comes to that, there is no doubt where the religious
spirit of our forefathers will force the majority to stand.
It is true, perhaps, that there is less outward observance
of religion than there was with our forefathers ; but the

religious spirit still remains, and the blessings which it prompted them to struggle for a century ago, it will not now allow corrupt politicians to destroy.

The celebration of this series of centennial anniversaries, which is about to begin, will but poorly honor the men who shed their blood on yonder Green, and those who followed them in their act of sacrifice, in all the colonies, if it ends with the noise of cannons, the roll of drums, and eloquent words. Unless it incites us to be more watchful of the blessings for which they gave their lives, more watchful against every foe, it seems as if their sleeping dust must cry out *shame*! We would call ourselves unworthy descendants of them, if without resistance we allowed a foreign enemy to deprive us of the liberty which they obtained. Are we any less unworthy if we allow the dishonesty and corruption of politicians to undermine the foundation of what they established? This celebration will be unworthy of this people unless it leads us to honor the virtues of our forefathers, and inspires us with more of that spirit of dependence upon God, as a nation, which they possessed; unless it leads us to make the Lord the God of our nation, through obedience of his laws. It will not be enough to place the name *God* in the constitution, for that would be only like the Jews, careful for the name of God, but careless about his spirit in the heart. The poet has said of the Ship of State, the Union:

> " We know what anvils rang, what hammers beat,
>   In what a forge and what a heat
>   Were shaped the anchors of thy hope."

We have seen that those anchors of hope came from the

forge of the church, and the heat of religious enthusiasm ; and the more we make our anchor of hope now that religion which consists in obedience of the laws of God, the more certain shall we be that the next century of our national existence will be brighter than the past.

A SERMON DELIVERED APRIL 25TH, 1875.

EXODUS XII, 14.

"THIS DAY SHALL BE UNTO YOU FOR A MEMORIAL; YE SHALL KEEP IT A FEAST BY AN ORDINANCE FOREVER." .

It has been a common custom among all nations to perpetuate the remembrance of heroic men and heroic deeds by some kind of memorial. The forms of heroic men have been carved in marble, or cast in metal; and the accounts of heroic deeds have been inscribed on the same enduring substances. The cities of Athens and Rome were noted for the great number of such memorials which they contained. In the early history of the Jews, we find accounts of this same custom, although observed in a much ruder manner. Jacob, after he had dreamed of the ladder with the angels ascending and descending, "rose up early in the morning," it is said, "and took the stone that he had put for his pillow, and set it up for a pillar, and poured oil upon the top of it." When the children of Israel passed through the river Jordan, Joshua commanded twelve men, one man out of each of the twelve tribes, to take each a stone from the bed of the river, and carry them to the land, and place them together, "that this," he said, "may be a sign among you, that when your children ask their fathers in time to come, saying, what mean ye by these stones, then ye shall answer them, 'That the waters of Jordan were cut off before the ark of the covenant of the Lord, and those stones shall be for a memorial unto the children of Israel for ever.'" In the same way the service of the passover was to be annually a memorial of the departure of the children of Israel from Egypt. "This day," said Moses, "shall be unto you for a memorial ; ye shall keep it a feast by an ordinance for ever. And when your children shall say unto you, what mean you by this service ; ye shall say, 'It is the sacrifice of the Lord's passover, who passed over the houses of the children of Israel in Egypt, when he smote the Egyptians, and delivered our houses.'"

No one can doubt that such memorials, whether expressed in metal or stone, or in the observance of a day, serve a very important purpose in the life of a nation. They keep alive the memory of those who labored and suffered for the nation ; they keep fresh in the thoughts the heroic deeds of the past, all of which tends to increase the spirit of patriotism in the hearts of the people. So long as the people of a nation cherish the memory of its founders and sustainers, no danger can threaten the existence of the nation, without arousing multitudes for national defence. The Jews were careful to observe the passover, the memorial of their deliverance from Egypt ; and although they were finally conquered, and destroyed as a nation, yet there is no doubt that the custom which still remains wherever a remnant of them can be found, of observing this annual memorial feast, serves to keep them distinct from every other nation, although they are scattered over every part of the world.

Our annual celebration of the declaration of American Independence has been of immense value to this nation.

We are apt to smile at the noisy demonstrations and exultant orations of the Fourth of July; but although we may be a little critical of the manner in which the day is observed, this nation can not well afford to dispense with the celebration of that important event in our history. As the Jewish children asked concerning the observance of the passover, " What mean ye by this service ? " so have the children in this country asked the same concerning this annual celebration, and they have learned its meaning; and its noise and tumult have made an impression on every boy's heart. That readiness with which men in every part of the land, in 1861, answered the call to take up arms in defence of our national existence had its foundation in Fourth-of-July celebrations. May the time never come when the day will cease to be observed in some appropriate manner. When the Fourth of July ceases to be an exceptional day in our national calendar, we may begin to tremble at the fate of our nation.

The events which occurred in this town, and of which we have just celebrated the centennial anniversary, were not unlike, in spirit at least, the event which Moses commanded the Jews to observe by a memorial day. With the Jews, it was their departure from the territory of a nation who held them as slaves; on the nineteenth of April, 1775, began that series of events which resulted in driving from this land those who were endeavoring to make slaves of the colonists. And if there were any good reason why that day should be unto the Jews for a memorial, why it should be kept a feast by an ordinance for ever, there is equally good reason why the nineteenth of April should be unto our nation for a memorial, and should be kept a feast by an ordinance forever. If we have had doubts of this heretofore, I think the celebration which has occurred during the past week has laid all such doubts at rest.

There may have been some persons who thought that the significance of this celebration was greatly magnified in the eyes of the citizens of Lexington. But looking back upon it now, we know very well that our ideas of its importance and significance did not exceed similar ideas which were entertained in every part of this country. Very few of us, I think, fully realized what a great manifestation of interest in the day would be exhibited. From every part of this country we have had evidence that there was a deep interest in the observance of the day, and that the day was observed not only in this and our neighboring town, but in many other towns of this Commonwealth, and in many States of the Union. So large a concourse of people as assembled here last Monday, hardly any one of the most sanguine of our citizens expected to see. And when we remember that half as many more tried in vain to reach Lexington on that day, we must feel that such a manifestation of interest in any patriotic occasion has seldom been surpassed. The character and conduct of the crowd was also equally remarkable. A very small proportion of the number who participated in the celebration, or who endeavored so to do, was composed of the element termed rowdy. Very few indeed seemed drawn hither merely to see or form a part of a crowd. There were men of every profession, business, and occupation, apparently drawn hither from real interest in the event which was commemorated. Rev. Dr. Bel-

lows, who was unable to get any further on his way to
Lexington than Boston, and who returned to New York,
as he says, "baffled and sorely disappointed in the object
of his patriotic journey," also says that he was "partly
repaid by the immense exhibition of interest and zeal
in the occasion which the crowd displayed." And I
think this must be especially gratifying to every one
who either saw or heard of it. Last Monday was the
beginning of a series of centennial anniversaries which
are to be observed during the coming period of eight
years. And the great interest displayed in this first
anniversary of the series shows with what deep interest
and reverence the American people regard the struggle
which our forefathers endured, in order to establish this
nation upon the solid foundation of political and religious liberty. In February, 1775, both houses of the
English Parliament joined in an address to the king,
declaring that a rebellion existed in Massachusetts, and
pledging their lives and properties to its suppression.
During the discussion which took place upon that
address, John Wilkes said : " Who can tell whether, in
consequence of this day's violent and mad address, the
scabbard may not be thrown away by the Americans as
well as by us ; and, should success attend them, whether,
in a few years, the Americans may not celebrate the
glorious era of the revolution of 1775, as we do that of
1688 ? " His words proved to be the words of a true
prophet ; and now, after a century has passed away, the
American people have entered upon the celebration of
that "glorious era" with renewed interest and zeal,
giving evidence not only of the honor which is felt to
be due to the men of that era, but also of the value

which is attached to what, by their labors, by their struggles, and by their sacrifices, they obtained.

But besides this manifestation of patriotism which the celebration of the anniversary of the battle of Lexington and Concord has produced, and that which will be shown on the anniversaries which are to follow, there is another thing which it seems to me every person must feel will result therefrom; and that is, the strengthening of that bond of political union among the different States which has, of late years, suffered so severe a strain. Very few, after our late domestic struggle, could say of it what Longfellow said before :

> " 'Tis but the flapping of the sail,
> And not a rent made by the gale!"

It was a rent, and a very serious one ; and since the rent has been repaired, it has been the earnest wish of every lover of his country to see all traces of it removed, and the old feeling of union replaced, as strong and firm as ever. Can any one doubt that the celebration of these centennial anniversaries, which have been so auspiciously begun, and in which men from every State in the Union will join, will tend to strengthen that old feeling of unity which has been so seriously disturbed ? Will it be possible for men from every part of this country to meet together in order to honor the men who one hundred years ago laid the foundation of this Union, without being more deeply impressed with the value of what our forefathers established ? As pilgrims from the South and pilgrims from the North meet together in places made sacred by the deliberations or sacrifices of our forefathers, the clasping of their hands

48

must be a true symbol of the renewed feeling of union with which they will return to their homes.

A poet has told the story of a husband and wife, after long years of wilful separation, meeting at the grave of their child, where memories of former days of love and happiness came thronging upon them, and there they pledged anew their mutual faith and trust in each other. When North and South meet at such places as Lexington, Concord, Bunker Hill, Philadelphia, Trenton, Princetown, Eutaw, and Yorktown, to honor the dead, in whom both North and South have a mutual interest, the thronging memories connected with these places must revive, to a great degree, the old feeling of union, and make them again regard themselves as "one and inseparable." Therefore, when I think of the proceedings of last Monday, and ask myself what was the grandest part of those exercises, I pass by that grand procession. I say, not those eloquent introductory words of the president of the day; not that thrilling scene of the unveiling of the statues of the patriots, Adams and Hancock; not that eloquent, beautiful and masterly oration, but the last part of the speech of the Governor of South Carolina. If the celebration had accomplished nothing more than the bringing of the Governor of South Carolina to give utterance to those words on the soil of Lexington, it would have been a grand success. It was a part of the day's exercises which I was unfortunate enough not to hear, and it has been difficult for me to read it since without feeling tears of joy starting in my eyes. The words of which I speak are these:

"I know that I am commissioned here to-day to say

for South Carolina that she joins with equal gratitude and reverence with all her sisters of the early days in honoring the nineteenth of April, 1775 ; that she claims her share in the glory of the struggle begun at Lexington ; that as of old she bade Massachusetts cheer in the struggle, so now she unites with her in these patriotic services.

"It is not for me, it is not for any one, on this occasion, to speak of later events in which these two ancient allies stood face to face as enemies. Who that has an American heart does not rejoice that, back of all the recent bitter struggle, there lies the gracious heritage of those common labors and dangers and sacrifices in founding this common government? Who that looks with a just eye even on that recent struggle does not now see, on either side, the same high elements of character, the courage, the devotion to duty, the moral lineaments of the Adamses and Hancocks, the Gadsdens and Rutledges of a hundred years ago? Who that has faith in the destinies of America does not see in this early friendship,—aye, and even in this later conflict, the potency and promise of that coming Union under whose protection liberty shall forever walk hand in hand with justice, wherein the North and the South, reunited in spirit and aims, shall again respond to every call of patriotic duty in the old tones of Samuel Adams and Christopher Gadsden, of James Otis and John Rutledge?

"That spirit still lives, fellow-citizens, in South Carolina. If in later days she has erred, forgive her ; for even then she dared and suffered with a courage and patience not unworthy in its strength of the days when Gadsden and Rutledge illustrated her civic wisdom, and

Sumter and Marion her martial prowess. 'Magnanim-
ity,' says Mr. Burke, 'is not seldom the truest wisdom;
and a great empire and little minds go ill together.'

"Fellow-citizens, I offer you to-day the fraternal,
patriotic greetings of South Carolina—of *all* her people.
She marches again to-day to the music of that Union
which a hundred years ago her wisdom helped to de-
vise and her blood to cement. There, in that hallowed
Union, endeared and sanctified by so many blessed
memories, and radiant with so many proud hopes and
promises, there, there 'she must live or bear no life.'
Oh, welcome her anew to-day to the old fellowship!
The monuments of marble and brass which we raise
here to-day will crumble. Let us, therefore, build in
the hearts of all the people that imperishable monument,
'an indestructible Union of indestructible States.'"

Let such words find an echo at every centennial celebration which is to follow during the next eight years,
and these celebrations will effect almost as much of
good as did the war which they are intended to com-
memorate. Let the spirit of those words prevail at
these centennials, and it seems impossible that it should
not; and then, when in 1883 we celebrate the centennial anniversary of the signing of a treaty of peace
between Great Britian and the United States, we shall
also celebrate the re-union, both in word and spirit, of
the nation. Then will every State again join in the
words of the poet:

"Thou, too, sail on, Oh Ship of State!
Sail on, Oh Union, strong and great!
Sail on, nor fear to breast the sea!
Our hearts, our hopes, are all with thee,
Our hearts, our hopes, our prayers, our tears,
Our faith triumphant o'er our fears,
Are all with thee,—are all with thee!"

I have mentioned these two things first,—this manifestation of the patriotic spirit, and the probable strengthening of the feeling of union, as results of this and the following centennial celebrations,—because they are of the greatest importance, being national in their character. But there is something which the recent surprising manifestation of interest in our centennial anniversary should teach us as citizens of this town. It is this: that the citizens of this historic town have a duty to perform on account of the interest which centres here. The whole country, as we have seen, feels an interest in the associations and memories which cluster around this place. Those who live in the town are the guardians of that interest. The man who stays in this town, and takes no interest in the associations and memories of the place, is not worthy to be called a citizen of Lexington. He is no citizen of the town. As guardians of the national interest in Lexington, it is our duty to preserve and increase that interest, not for the honor of the town, but for the benefit of the nation. The deeper and wider the interest in the associations and memories of this place, the deeper and wider is the spirit of patriotism. The way to perform the duty which we owe to the country, as citizens of Lexington, is not to heed the advice which some editor, during the past week, has been obliging enough to give to both Lexington and Concord; that is, " turn over and take another nap of a hundred years." We ought to do just the opposite to that; we ought to keep awake to the national interest in, and historic character of, the town. One way to do this, is never to let the nineteenth of April pass without some observance of the day. We who have witnessed this celebration will never witness another like it. But the exceptional character of this celebration should not prevent our taking some notice of the day every year. Let there be, at least, the national banner displayed on every house, and such other simple observance as will be inexpensive, and at the same time affording pleasure. Such a yearly celebration will not only strengthen the spirit of patriotism in this town, but all over the land. The news of such an observance would go from one end of the land to the other, and children would ask what is meant by it, and thus learn the story, and take in the spirit of the day.

Another way to perform our duty is to preserve the historic character of the town in its outward appearance. The names of the streets should be historic. They should be such that a stranger losing his way and coming into this village would know from the names on the sign-boards that he must be in Lexington, and could not possibly be any where else. And we may keep the historic character of the town, outwardly, by preserving the old historic houses. If it be necessary, let there be an association formed for this purpose. People are always interested in old houses. Some one told me, last Monday, that the most eloquent motto was on the house just below here : " A witness of the battle one hundred years ago." One of the great objects of interest to visitors will always be the old houses which stood here witnesses of the battle. Let us see that they are preserved, so that they may speak to every stranger visitor, eloquently, although silently, of the spirit of the men of 1775.

Another way to do our duty in this historic town is

to preserve all the relics which illustrate in any way its history. Such things are also eloquent and interesting teachers of the past. One newspaper correspondent who was in Lexington last Monday says, "I for one enjoy seeing an old foot-stove, with which a venerable dame, a hundred years ago, mitigated the severity of a winter atmosphere in the meeting-house, or the blanket in which Sam Adams was christened, more than the military display, or the President and his Cabinet." Such relics are of interest to most people, and they are a real source of patriotic inspiration. Let that part of the collection in our library which has been given to the town, be increased till it shall come to be such a collection as every lover of antiquities will never visit Boston without coming to Lexington to see. In such ways as these, and in others which may suggest themselves, let us prove to the country that we are not asleep, but awake to the historic and patriotic interest in our town.

Of the seven men of Lexington who were killed on the green, on the morning of the nineteenth of April, 1765, Bancroft says : "Their names are held in grateful remembrance, and the expanding millions of their countrymen renew and multiply their praise from generation to generation," and his words during the past week have been proved true. Let us remember that it is the duty of the citizens of this town to do what they can to keep alive the memories of those men, not for the honor of Lexington, not solely for their honor, but for the good of our nation, to establish which on the firm foundation of liberty they sacrificed their lives.

www.ingramcontent.com/pod-product-compliance
Lightning Source LLC
Chambersburg PA
CBHW031801090426
42739CB00008B/1114